Great Moments in
Olympic
GYMNASTICS

By Blythe Lawrence

SportsZone

An Imprint of Abdo Publishing
www.abdopublishing.com

www.abdopublishing.com

Published by Abdo Publishing, a division of ABDO, PO Box 398166, Minneapolis, Minnesota 55439. Copyright © 2015 by Abdo Consulting Group, Inc. International copyrights reserved in all countries. No part of this book may be reproduced in any form without written permission from the publisher. SportsZone™ is a trademark and logo of Abdo Publishing.

Printed in the United States of America, North Mankato, Minnesota
042014
092014

Cover Photo: Margaret Bowles/AP Images
Interior Photos: Margaret Bowles/AP Images, 1, 52–53; Michel Lipchitz/AP Images, 6–7; Paul Vathis/AP Images, 10; AP Images, 12–13, 15, 23; Lionel Cironneau/AP Images, 17, 18–19; Marc Francotte/TempSport/Corbis, 24–25; Craig Fujii/AP Images, 29; Santiago Lyon/AP Images, 30–31; Ales Fevzer/Corbis, 33; John Gaps III/AP Images, 36; Kevork Djansezian/AP Images, 38–39; Amy Sancetta/AP Images, 42; Matt Dunham/AP Images, 44–45, 48, 55; Dick Druckman/AP Images, 51; Gregory Bull/AP Images, 56; Julie Jacobson/AP Images, 59

Editor: Chrös McDougall
Series Designer: Craig Hinton

Library of Congress Control Number: 2014932859

Cataloging-in-Publication Data
Lawrence, Blythe.
 Great moments in Olympic gymnastics / Blythe Lawrence.
   p. cm. -- (Great moments in Olympic sports)
Includes bibliographical references and index.
ISBN 978-1-62403-394-0
1. Gymnastics--Juvenile literature. 2. Olympics--Juvenile literature.   I. Title.
796.41--dc23

                                                    2014932859

Contents

Introduction

The ancient Greeks were the first to do gymnastics. However, modern gymnastics like we know today began in the 1800s in Germany. The sport was seen as an activity to help men and women stay healthy and strong. Artistic gymnastics is the most popular form of gymnastics. And it has been a part of every modern Olympic Games since the first one, in 1896.

Olympic gymnastics has greatly changed over the years. Only men competed in Olympic gymnastics until 1928. Some early

Olympic gymnastics events included rope climbing and club swinging. The modern gymnastics programs were finalized during the 1950s. Women compete in balance beam, floor exercise, uneven bars, and vault. Men compete in floor exercise, high bar, parallel bars, pommel horse, still rings, and vault. Men and women also have an all-around competition and a team competition. Rhythmic gymnastics has been an Olympic event since 1984. Trampoline debuted in the 2000 Games.

In the past, artistic gymnasts aimed to score a perfect 10. However, the scoring system changed in 2006. Gymnasts now receive two scores for each event. One is for difficulty and the other is execution. Those scores are combined. There is no longer a perfect score. A great score today is in the 15s or 16s.

1

Montreal 1976
PERFECTION

In 1976, Nadia Comaneci was a girl among women. She was in Montreal, Canada, about to compete in her first Olympic Games. But at age 14, she was younger than most of the other gymnasts. She was smaller, too. Comaneci stood just 4 feet 11 inches tall. She weighed only 86 pounds.

Today's Olympic women's gymnasts are often teenagers. That was not the case in the decades before. For years, gymnastics was considered a sport best suited for adults. But that idea was beginning to change.

Nadia Comaneci of Romania performs on the balance beam at the 1976 Olympic Games in Montreal, Canada.

Younger and lighter gymnasts were taking over. And Comaneci's coaches were leading the charge.

Bela Karolyi and his wife Martha Karolyi began coaching gymnastics in the 1960s in Deva, Romania. The coaches pushed their students to master original skills. They emphasized daring skills as well. Before long, their gym was getting attention. Their young gymnasts were finding success at many junior level competitions. Romania, meanwhile, was emerging as a gymnastics power.

Comaneci was one of the Karolyis' first students. Bela had noticed her on her school playground in 1967. The kindergartner was turning cartwheels. Bela recognized her potential. He invited her to train with him in Deva.

The Youth Movement

There had been rumblings of change in gymnastics even before Nadia Comaneci. One big sign came in 1972. That year's Olympics were held in Munich, West Germany. A perky 17-year-old Soviet named Olga Korbut captured the world's attention. She attempted skills nobody had ever thought possible. Korbut did a standing backflip on the balance beam. She also did the first-ever backward release move on the uneven bars. Korbut laid out a back flip from the top bar and then re-caught it. Her bravery won her gold medals on balance beam and floor exercise. Meanwhile, fans worldwide were attracted to her plucky, mischievous charm. Korbut helped prove that younger gymnasts could do more difficult skills with greater ease. Comaneci would become the example that solidified the rule.

Multiples of 10

Many believed the Soviet Union had the best women's gymnastics team in 1976. The Soviets featured defending Olympic all-around champion Lyudmila Turishcheva and 1972 Olympic darling Olga Korbut. But newcomer Comaneci's four gold-medal performance at the 1975 European Championships was a preview of things to come. She went on to win the all-around title at the first American Cup in New York City. That meet was held a few months before the Games. There, Comaneci had done something astounding. She scored a perfect 10 for her vault in the preliminary round. Then she scored another 10 on the floor exercise. The stage had been set for the Olympic Games.

The 1976 Olympic gymnastics competition began with team compulsory exercises. All of the gymnasts perform the same routines in that round. The optional round was held later. That is when each gymnast performs unique routines with a variety of skills.

Comaneci captured the moment. She flew through her compulsory routine on uneven bars. It was a difficult routine. But Comaneci made it look easy. She moved from bar to bar with ease. She flew through the air on her release moves. These are skills in which the gymnast lets go of the bar and soars through the air. When the judges posted her score, it

Nadia Comaneci dismounts from the uneven bars after her perfect routine at the 1976 Olympic Games.

seemed unbelievable. The scoreboard read: 1.00. It took a moment for everyone to realize what had happened. The Olympic scoreboards could not show a perfect score. Comaneci actually had scored 10.0. It was the first perfect score in Olympic gymnastics history.

Fans in the arena wildly applauded Comaneci. The gymnast hopped back onto the event platform and took a bow. Then she waved to the audience with all her might.

"I had tears in my eyes because it was so gorgeous," Bela Karolyi said of the routine.

The Olympic gymnastics competition was really just beginning. There were several more days of competition. And Comaneci never left the spotlight. She went on to score six more 10s. It was little surprise that she went home with a handful of medals. She won the women's all-around gold medal. Then she claimed individual gold medals on the uneven bars and balance beam. Her accomplishments made her an instant star in her native Romania. She quickly became a worldwide celebrity, too.

With a single routine, Comaneci had defined her sport. She also had changed it fundamentally. The gymnasts who followed her would be younger than before Comaneci's arrival. Their tricks would be harder. The athletes also would be thirstier for perfection. The sport of gymnastics would never be the same.

The Second Perfect 10

Nadia Comaneci was the biggest gymnastics star at the 1976 Olympics. But the Soviet women still won the team gold medal. Nineteen-year-old Nellie Kim was the team's leader. Her standout performance came in the women's all-around final. Kim stuck a marvelous Tsukahara vault with a full twist. The judges awarded her the second 10 in Olympic history. Kim also won gold medals on vault and floor exercise.

2

Los Angeles 1984
THE MIRACLE ON THE MATS

The 1980 Games were scheduled for Moscow, Soviet Union. That turned out to be a problem for Team USA. The United States opposed the 1979 Soviet invasion of Afghanistan and boycotted the Olympics. The US athletes stayed home. It was bitterly disappointing for the athletes. But there was hope for some of the younger athletes. The 1984 Olympics were scheduled for Los Angeles, California. US teammates Bart Conner, Jim Hartung, and Peter Vidmar kept training.

Team USA gymnast Bart Conner performs on the high bar at the 1984 Olympic Games in Los Angeles, California.

Becoming Champions

The gymnasts who would make up the 1984 US Olympic team got to know each other. They had all been college gymnasts. Hartung and Scott Johnson were from the University of Nebraska. Vidmar, Tim Daggett, and Mitch Gaylord competed for the University of California, Los Angeles. Conner hailed from the University of Oklahoma.

Few believed Team USA could win a gold medal at the 1984 Olympics. But Hartung was one of the believers. He saw what great talent he and his teammates had at the US Olympic Trials. Still, other teams were considered better. The Chinese won the team title at the World Championships in 1983. They had knocked the strong Soviet team from

Moscow Magic

The first perfect 10 in Olympic men's gymnastics was awarded in 1980. There was no singular moment as famous as Nadia Comaneci's in 1976. However, five men received perfect scores at the Games in Moscow, Soviet Union. The great Soviet gymnast Alexander Dityatin received a 10 on vault. He won a stunning eight medals in Moscow. Fellow Soviet Alexander Tkatchev was judged to be perfect on the high bar. He is famous for inventing the popular release skill that bears his name. Bulgaria's Stoyan Deltchev received his 10 on rings. East German Michael Nikolay was flawless on the pommel horse. But he did not win gold. Hungary's Zoltan Magyar had won the pommel horse in 1976. He defended his title in 1980 while scoring 10 twice along the way.

Tim Daggett of the United States performs a skill on the rings at the 1984 Olympic Games.

the top spot on the podium. The Americans hadn't even won a medal. That did little to deter Hartung.

"We can beat China," he told his new Olympic teammates.

Hartung's teammates began to believe, too. The Americans would be competing at home. They had worked very hard. It could be their moment, Hartung urged. All they had to do was take it. Then the news broke that the Soviet Union was boycotting the Los Angeles Games. That took a major obstacle out of Team USA's path.

The Olympic competition began with team compulsories. The Americans got off to a strong start. Many were surprised to see Team USA finish the round 1.05 points ahead of China. The optional round was next. The Chinese team was known for the difficulty and beauty of its exercises. But the Americans were up to the challenge.

The team round got off to a special start for the Americans. Gaylord had been the country's top-ranked gymnast in 1983 and 1984. He stepped up in Los Angeles and did the rings routine of his life. He ended it with a perfectly executed half-in half-out dismount. His reward was a 10. It was the first 10 by a US man at an Olympic Games.

The United States and China seesawed during the next several events. It all came down to the final rotation. Team USA's last event was the high bar. It was especially dangerous for Gaylord. He was the third gymnast to compete. And he performed one of the most difficult release skills in the competition. The move was a flip over the bar with a half twist. Gaylord's coach, Abie Grossfeld, was weary. He knew that Gaylord was only successful about 75 percent of the time on that move.

Grossfeld considered asking Gaylord not to do his most difficult skill. But Grossfeld's gut told him to let Gaylord take the chance. On the bar, Gaylord released perfectly. He then flipped over the bar and made a

From left, Americans Bart Conner, Peter Vidmar, Jim Hartung, Mitch Gaylord, Scott Johnson, and Tim Daggett won the Olympic gold medal in 1984.

spectacular catch. The rest of the routine was flawless. Gaylord stuck his dismount to a roar from the crowd.

After that, there was no stopping Team USA. Conner, Daggett, and Vidmar all turned in excellent performances. The team gold medal was secured.

The medal was so unexpected that the media dubbed the event "The Miracle on the Mats." But it wasn't a miracle. It was reality. And it had all started with a belief.

Los Angeles 1984
AN AMERICAN FIRST

Nadia Comaneci's performance had changed many things in the sport. Suddenly, gymnasts had to do much harder skills to be competitive. Comaneci, the Soviets, and the Chinese kept pushing the limits. They introduced new elements in every event. Each new skill seemed more difficult than the last.

It would take a special gymnast to compete against the world's best. That special gymnast soon emerged in West Virginia. Mary Lou Retton had three qualities that made gymnasts successful. She was short, strong, and

Mary Lou Retton became the United States' biggest gymnastics star following her performance at the 1984 Olympic Games in Los Angeles, California.

stubborn. Retton had a tiny but muscular body. She did not look like the elegant Eastern European champions. But she had explosive power in her tumbling and vaulting. Plus, she had a spark to her gymnastics. Fans were drawn to her performances.

Meanwhile, Bela and Martha Karolyi were not happy in Romania. The famous coaches decided to make a new life in the United States. They moved in 1981. The coaches settled in Texas. They bought land and built a large gym. There, the coaches could train their own athletes. One of those athletes was Retton. The young gymnast moved to Texas to train with Bela. Retton dedicated herself wholly to training for the Olympics. She even stopped attending high school. Instead, she did her schooling through the mail.

The "Alternate Olympics"

The Soviets were not happy when Team USA boycotted the 1980 Olympic Games. They got payback in 1984. The Soviet Union and several allies decided to boycott the 1984 Games in Los Angeles, California. Those countries still wanted to showcase their athletes, though. So they held their own alternate competition. It was called the Friendship Games. The event was held in what is known today as the Czech Republic. Soviet gymnast Olga Mostepanova was the star of the Friendship Games. She won the women's all-around title by scoring a 10 on every event.

Retton's big break came in the spring of 1983. US champion Dianne Durham was injured a few days before the American Cup. Organizers asked Retton to replace Durham. Retton didn't waste her chance. She won the title outright. That instantly established her as a serious Olympic contender. Meanwhile in Europe, a new Romanian champion was emerging. Ecaterina Szabo won five medals at the 1983 World Championships. She scored 10s on vault and floor exercise. She too seemed on track for Olympic glory.

Showdown in Los Angeles

Fans eagerly awaited the gymnastics showdown at the 1984 Olympic Games. The all-around competition was shaping up to be one for the ages. Szabo began on balance beam and scored a 10. She followed with an almost perfect exercise on floor. Retton, however, got off to a slow start in the uneven bars and balance beam.

Retton was gaining confidence with each event, though. She knew her floor exercise routine would be key. Without a great performance, her dreams of Olympic gold would be lost. Like a rocket, she launched herself into her first tumbling pass. She nailed the double layout. Retton capped her routine by sticking the landing on her final pass. The judges were bowled over by such a display of energy. They awarded her a 10.

Szabo went to the uneven bars for her final routine. It was her weakest event. But she battled through without making a major error. The judges gave her a 9.9. That set the stage for Retton on vault. She would need to score a 10 to win the gold medal. Anything less, and Szabo would win.

Retton set herself at the edge of the vault runway. There was a look of intense concentration in her brown eyes. Everything she had trained for had come down to this one moment. She didn't hesitate. Retton launched herself down the runway. Then she exploded off the springboard and into the air.

Retton pushed off the vault table. Her body stretched into a perfect layout position as she spun into a full twist. And in an instant it was over. She landed lightly, her feet sticking to the mat. An exclamation

Rhythmic Rolls into the Olympics

The 1984 Olympic Games were the first to feature rhythmic gymnastics. Rhythmic gymnasts perform routines using five different apparatus. They are the rope, the ball, the clubs, the hoop, and the ribbon. The sport was developed and remains extremely popular in Eastern Europe. However, many of those countries ended up boycotting the first Olympic Games to feature the sport. The first Olympic rhythmic gymnastics champion in history was Lori Fung of Canada.

American Mary Lou Retton performs in the uneven bars finals at the 1984 Olympic Games.

of joy escaped from her lips as she lifted her arms into the air. Retton began jumping up and down. It was the best vault she had ever done. Overjoyed, she ran off the mat and into Bela's arms.

The judges didn't take long to calculate the score. A "10" flashed on the scoreboard. Retton had won the Olympic gold medal.

Retton's performance made US history. The Eastern Europeans had long dominated the sport. In fact, no American woman had ever won an Olympic all-around medal until Retton. And she did it on home soil.

Barcelona 1992
THE HIGH FLIER

The 1992 Olympic Games were held in Barcelona, Spain. US Olympic men's gymnastics coach Ed Burch made a prediction for what fans of his team should expect there. "Our high bar will stand out," he said.

He could not have known how right he was.

The Olympic Games are known for producing unexpected outcomes. Sometimes an unknown athlete has the performance of his or her life. And sometimes, that performance is good enough for gold. Trent Dimas was one of those athletes. He began gymnastics

Team USA's Trent Dimas performs on the high bar at the 1992 Olympic Games in Barcelona, Spain.

because he liked watching cartoons. Gymnasts fly through the air like cartoon super heroes. And in no event do male gymnasts fly higher than on the high bar. That quickly became Dimas's favorite event. He loved performing release skills.

Dimas failed to make the 1988 US Olympic team. That did not discourage him, though. Dimas resumed training. He tried out again, four years later, for the 1992 Olympic team. This time, Dimas finished fifth at the US Olympic Trials. That was good enough to make the six-person squad.

An Unexpected Star

Dimas was a well-balanced gymnast. His best event was the high bar. But he was not one of the stars of the American team. Even Dimas did not expect to win a medal in Barcelona.

The Soviet Union's government had dissolved one year earlier, in 1991. The former Soviet athletes performed in 1992 under the new label of the Unified Team. Those athletes lived up to their high expectations. Vitaly Scherbo proved to be the men's gymnastics star in Barcelona. "The Man from Minsk" led the Unified Team to the gold medal. Then he captured the men's all-around title. But he was only getting started. Scherbo won the parallel bars, pommel horse, still rings, and vault. That meant he took six of the possible eight gold medals in men's gymnastics. Only one athlete had ever won more gold medals in one Olympics. Scherbo's only weakness happened to be on high bar. That was the only event in which he did not qualify for the individual final.

The Barcelona Olympics were difficult for the US men. The magic of 1984's "Miracle on the Mats" had faded. Members of that team had since retired. The next generation struggled to build upon that momentum. The US men finished sixth as a team in Barcelona. The top American finished nineteenth in the all-around competition. A few US gymnasts qualified

From Soviet to Russian

The Soviet Union produced many great gymnasts. They were often known as much for style and grace as for big skills. However, two of the greatest Soviet gymnasts competed after that country dissolved in 1991. Vitaly Scherbo won six gold medals at the 1992 Olympics for the Unitied Team. Then he won four bronze medals for Belarus at 1996 Olympics in Atlanta, Georgia. Russia's Alexei Nemov then became the prince of post-Soviet gymnastics. Nemov trained under the Soviet system as a boy. He has been called the "last of the Soviets." The charismatic performer debuted at the 1996 Olympics. There, he helped Russia win a surprise team gold medal. Four years later, he won the all-around gold medal in Sydney, Australia. Through 2012, he was the only Russian man to win that title. Nemov retired after the 2004 Olympics. He had won 12 medals, including four golds.

for event finals. But nobody had won a medal through five rotations. High bar was the only event left.

Dimas had not expected to make the high bar final. However, his high-flying release moves had impressed the judges. Dimas performed a Kovacs, which is a double back flip before catching the bar again. He also did a daring triple back somersault dismount. The judges scored his routine 9.725. Dimas had the sixth-best score. That was good enough to make the event finals.

Getting into the medal round was one thing. Winning a medal would be harder. Scherbo was not in the final. But his teammate Grigory Misutin was a favorite to win gold. Germany's Andreas Wecker would challenge for gold, too. Both scored 9.837.

Dimas struggled in his warm-up routine. But when he began his actual performance, all of his years of training seemed to take over. Dimas

Multiple Medalists

No gymnast through 2012 had come close to matching Vitaly Scherbo's six gold medals in one Olympic Games. The Soviet Union's Larisa Latynina still held the record for career gymnastics medals. She won 18 medals over three Olympic Games from 1956 to 1964. Nine of those medals were gold. In fact, Latynina's 18 medals was long an all-time Olympic record. However, US swimmer Michael Phelps surpassed that record at the 2012 Olympics.

Trent Dimas of the United States celebrates after winning a gold medal on high bar at the 1992 Olympic Games.

swung through skill after skill with perfect form. He made it look easy. He released the bar to do his Kovacs. Then he re-caught the bar in perfect time to swing out. Soon there was only the dismount left. Dimas released the bar. He flipped through the air—once, twice, three times. Finally he landed on the ground. His feet didn't move. He had stuck the landing.

Dimas was shocked. The arena was in an uproar. This unknown American had delivered what fans thought was the best routine of the final. A moment later, the judges posted the score. They agreed. Dimas had received a 9.875. Coach Ed Burch's prediction had been right after all. Dimas went home from those Olympics with a gold medal.

Atlanta 1996
THE MAGNIFICENT SEVEN

The story of "The Magnificent Seven" really begins in 1992. The US team at the Barcelona Olympics was young, but full of potential. The squad won a bronze medal. Fifteen-year-old Shannon Miller added two individual silver and two bronze medals. And she was not going away. Neither were teammates Dominique Dawes and Kerri Strug. Miller, Dawes, and Strug were not satisfied with the team bronze. They felt like they could have performed better. They vowed to stay around until the 1996 Olympics.

Shannon Miller was the star of the US women's team at the 1992 Olympic Games in Barcelona, Spain.

Miller continued to improve over the next four years. She had been the star in Barcelona. Her consistency and focus were unmatched in the years after. Soon she started winning more and more championships. The biggest wins were in 1993 and 1994. Miller won the all-around title at the World Championships both years.

Dawes was right behind Miller. She improved rapidly after the 1992 Olympics. Sometimes Dawes showed inconsistency in international tournaments. But her flair made her a star. So did her performance at the 1994 US championships. Dawes swept all of the gold medals.

Strug had the most unusual road to her second Olympics. She had been training with coaches Bela and Martha Karolyi. But they retired after the 1992 Olympics. Strug needed to find a new coach. That quest took her all over the country. Strug tried gyms in Oklahoma, Arizona, and Colorado. But nothing felt quite right.

Then Bela Karolyi had a change of heart. In 1995, he reopened his gym in Texas. A very young gymnast named Dominique Moceanu began training there. She was a rising star in the sport. Soon, Strug joined her. Training with Bela was difficult. But Strug knew that he could help her achieve her potential.

Team USA's Dominique Dawes performs on the balance beam during the 1996 Olympic Games.

Miller, Strug, Dawes, and Moceanu all made the 1996 Olympic team. Olympic gymnastics squads had seven athletes at the time. The veteran Amanda Borden, the multitalented Amy Chow, and Jaycie Phelps also made the team.

The seven young women had one goal. They wanted to better the team result from 1992. Also, the 1996 Olympics were being held in Atlanta, Georgia. It meant a lot to each member of the team to perform well in front of the home crowd.

Dazzling the Home Crowd

The Soviet Union had long been a power in women's gymnastics. Since 1952, the only time the Soviet Union or Unified Team did not win the team gold medal was in 1984, when the country boycotted the Games. The Soviet Union had split into many different countries by 1996. The biggest of those countries was Russia. And the Russians came into the 1996 Olympics as the favorites to win the team title.

The Americans believed they could win, though. And they sensed their chance as soon as team finals began. The crowd inside Atlanta's Georgia Dome was wildly supportive. Fans loudly cheered for Team USA. The noise proved to be a distraction for some of the other gymnasts. Some of them even broke concentration and made mistakes. Team USA seemed to feed off the excitement. The Americans soared through the uneven bars, balance beam, and floor exercise. They hit every routine. Only one event remained. It was clear that Team USA could win the gold medal if the gymnasts did well on vault.

Six gymnasts each performed two vaults. The better of the two scores counted toward the team score. The best five scores from each team counted toward the team total. That meant one score could be dropped without hurting the team.

Fans inside the Georgia Dome roared with excitement as the rotation started. The first four Americans performed excellent vaults. Up next was Moceanu. She would have a chance to secure the team gold medal. All she had to do was land her vaults. Then something surprising happened. She fell on both attempts. The team momentum seemed to screech to a halt. Everything now appeared up to the sixth and final gymnast: Strug. Then she fell on her first vault as well. The US gymnasts could almost see the gold medal disappearing.

Strug, however, had other things to think about. She had fallen hard. Now her left ankle was hurting. She didn't know it yet, but she had torn two ligaments in her ankle. Regardless, Strug limped back down the vault runway for her second attempt. Team USA's fate was on the line.

Shun Fujimoto's Sacrifice

The Japanese men were trying to hang onto the Olympic gold medal in 1976. The Soviets were challenging hard. To make things worse, Japan's Shun Fujimoto had broken his kneecap competing on floor exercise. To ensure the team gold, however, Fujimoto was needed to compete on rings. He got through the routine. He even completed the dismount. Fujimoto flipped from a height of 7 feet (2.13 m) and landed on his broken knee. His 9.7 score helped ensure Japan would win gold. When asked years later whether he would do it all over again, Fujimoto was candid. "No, I would not," he said.

US coach Bela Karolyi carries injured Kerri Strug to the award ceremony for the 1996 Olympic gymnastics team competition.

The squad would win gold if she completed a successful vault. If not, the Russians would still have a shot.

Bela Karolyi saw that Strug was hurt. "Kerri, listen to me!" he called to her. "You can do it!" Strug didn't hesitate. She readied herself for her second vault. She stared straight ahead at the springboard. Somehow, she blocked out the pain. Then she zoomed down the runway.

Strug launched herself off the springboard and flew through the air. Her vault was a Yurchenko with one and a half twists. She had done it thousands of times in practice. And she did it again in Atlanta. Strug performed the vault marvelously. The landing was the key, though. Strug landed with both feet firmly on the ground. Her left foot immediately lifted off the ground as she hopped sideways to salute the judges. That signaled she had completed the vault.

Strug had successfully landed the vault. Team USA had won gold. But the landing had been too much for her ankle. The gymnast fell to the mat. The pain showed in her face. Two coaches had to help her limp off the mat. The Americans had won, but Strug's Olympics were over.

The medal ceremony was set to take place right away. But the US gymnasts did not want to go on the podium without Strug. Finally, there was a commotion in the arena. Strug appeared—in Karolyi's arms. They made their way toward the podium. Strug's teammates helped her hop onto the top step. The Magnificent Seven stood proudly as the Olympic gold medals were placed around their necks. It was an Olympic moment that had been four years in the making.

Magnificent Moments

Kerri Strug's vault stole the show for Team USA at the 1996 Olympics. But several members of the Magnificent Seven had great individual performances as well. Shannon Miller won her long-anticipated first gold medal when she won the balance beam. Amy Chow tied for silver on uneven bars. In addition, Dominique Dawes won bronze on the floor exercise.

ATHENS 2004 🞊🞊🞊🞊🞊

Athens 2004
GOLD AMONG
THE RUINS

The 2004 Olympic Games were held in Athens, Greece. Fans were excited that the Olympics were returning to the country where the event was founded. US gymnastics fans, meanwhile, had reason to be excited as well. Behind twin brothers Paul and Morgan Hamm, the US men's team was as strong as ever. And individually, Paul Hamm had the ability to do something amazing. One year earlier, in 2003, he became the first US man to win an all-around world title.

Paul Hamm of the United States competes on vault during the men's team final at the 2004 Olympic Games in Athens, Greece.

The US men's team performed well in Athens. It won the silver medal, just behind Japan. That was the first time the US men had won a medal as a team since the "Miracle on the Mats" 20 years before. Paul Hamm delivered a clutch performance on the high bar in the team final. Upon re-catching the bar on a release trick, one of his hands slipped off. But Hamm held on with one hand to save the routine. Hamm felt at the top of his game. He was ready for the all-around finals.

Hamm performed well during the first three events in the all-around finals. He led the field at the halfway point of the competition. The unexpected happened on the next event, though. Hamm landed his vault

Ageless Wonders

Bulgarian Jordan Jovtchev competed in his first Olympics in 1992. He nearly retired after a mediocre performance in the 1996 Olympics at age 23. Instead, he moved to Oklahoma and began coaching. Still in great shape, Jovtchev returned to competition. He won two bronze medals at the 2000 Olympics and then a silver medal and a bronze in 2004. At the 2012 Olympics, Jovtchev was still going at age 39. No previous gymnast had competed in six Olympics. But two actually achieved that feat in 2012. Oksana Chusovitina helped the Unified Team win a gold medal in 1992. She competed in the 1996, 2000, and 2004 Olympics for her native Uzbekistan. Then she moved to Germany to seek medical treatment for her son. Wearing German colors, she competed in the 2008 and 2012 Olympics. Chusovitina was 37 in London. She even won a silver medal in vault in 2008.

on his feet. But he was short of rotation. He stumbled to the side. Hamm tried to regain his balance. But there was too much momentum pulling him sideways. He skidded to a stop off the mat, nearly sitting in a judge's lap. The audience in the arena was stunned.

So was Hamm. After that rotation, he sat in twelfth place. That's it, he thought. His opportunity to win the all-around gold medal appeared to have passed. Years of hard work had been dashed in a single vault. Then he shook himself off. Two rotations remained. He had to finish the competition.

Hamm ended his day on the parallel bars and the high bar. And that's when his luck began to change. He scored 9.837 on the parallel bars. That was among the best routines he had ever performed on that event. And the score rocketed him from twelfth to fourth place.

Still, a gold medal remained a long shot as he walked to the high bar. But luck stayed on Hamm's side. Several of the other contenders had errors in their performances. By the start of Paul's high-bar performance, he was back in contention for a gold medal. And by the time he stuck his dismount, his fate was sealed. When Paul's name came up, his coach Miles Avery rushed over. "Olympic champion!" he yelled. Hamm was overcome with disbelief. "No!" he exclaimed. "Yes!" Avery cried.

Paul Hamm, *center*, stands on the medal podium with South Korea's Kim Dae Eun, *left*, and Yang Tae Young for the 2004 Olympic all-around competition.

Controversial Ending

Hamm had edged out two gymnasts from South Korea to win gold. Hamm stood between Kim Dae Eun and Yang Tae Young on the podium as they received their medals. Afterward, however, Yang's coach complained. He said the judges had made a mistake calculating Yang's score on parallel bars. The correct score would have made Yang the gold medalist.

The controversy grew as the days went by. Fans and media members debated what Paul should do. Some said he should give his gold medal to Yang. Others believed Paul earned the medal fairly. The issue went all the way to the Court of Arbitration for Sport, which rules on international sports disputes. It decided that Paul could keep his medal.

The victory was bittersweet for Paul. Yes, he was an Olympic gold medalist. But he would not be remembered for what he had done in the gym to earn the medal. "I feel like I won it three times—in the competition, in the media, and also in court," Paul remarked afterward. "It's probably the most sought-after medal of all the Olympic Games ever."

Hamm's performance in Athens also had long-term consequences for gymnastics. In 2006, the sport adopted new, more objective scoring rules. The perfect 10 would be no more.

Another American Champion

Paul Hamm wasn't the only golden American gymnast at the Athens Olympics. Carly Patterson watched Hamm's comeback in the all-around. She was inspired. Then the spunky 16-year-old gymnast from Texas nailed four solid routines in the women's all-around. That propelled her to the gold medal over Russian veteran Svetlana Khorkina. Patterson became only the second female gymnast in US history to win the Olympic all-around title. She also helped Team USA win a silver medal.

7

Beijing 2008
DIFFICULTY
VERSUS ARTISTRY

They were two young American women with one Olympic dream. Both were supremely talented. And both had proven themselves in the years before the 2008 Olympic Games in Beijing, China. But the similarities ended there for Shawn Johnson and Nastia Liukin.

Liukin was born in Russia. A future in gymnastics seemed certain. Her father, Valeri, had been a great gymnast in the Soviet Union. He had won two gold medals at the 1988 Olympics. Her mother, Anna, was a

US gymnast Nastia Liukin performs on the uneven bars during the all-around finals at the 2008 Olympic Games in Beijing, China.

rhythmic gymnast. She won a world championship in 1987. The young family moved to Texas when Nastia was a baby. Her parents wanted to coach gymnastics there.

The family did not have much money. They couldn't even afford to hire a babysitter for Nastia. So they brought her to the gym. Little Nastia thought the gym was a giant playground. She grew up imitating the older gymnasts. Soon, Nastia no longer had to mimic the other girls. She was doing harder skills than they were. Her talent was shining through.

Gymnastics did not run in the Johnson family. But Shawn's parents soon turned to the sport for their young daughter. Shawn seemed to have endless energy as a kid. Her parents figured gymnastics might be a good outlet. They were in luck. A former gymnast named Liang Chow had come

Another Rivalry

The 1988 Olympics in Seoul, South Korea, featured another memorable rivalry. Yelena Shushunova was from the Soviet Union. Daniela Silivas was from Romania. They were unquestionably the two best of their generation. They had another similarity to Shawn Johnson and Nastia Liukin. Both gymnasts had remarkably different styles. Shushunova was powerful. Silivas was graceful. Their all-around battle was tight. Shushunova edged Silivas with an excellent performance on vault. Silivas, however, came back with a strong showing in the event finals. She won gold medals on uneven bars, balance beam, and floor exercise.

from China to study English. The man everyone called Chow had stayed to open a gymnastics school near Johnson's home in Iowa. One day, Shawn's mom brought her to the gym. Smiling little Shawn jumped right onto the uneven bars. No question about it, she had found her sport.

Coaches could see great potential in Liukin and Johnson from an early age. But the two gymnasts had little in common. Johnson was tiny, muscular, and full of energy. She would flip and twist her way through her routines. Even the toughest acrobatics looked easy. Liukin couldn't do all of the flips and twists that Johnson could. But she was very precise technically. Liukin's execution scores were often higher.

The rivalry truly began in 2007, when Johnson joined Liukin on the senior national team. But Liukin was battling an ankle injury. She did not perform at her best. Meanwhile, Johnson easily won the US all-around title. Then she became the world all-around champion a few weeks later.

Despite her injuries, Liukin won the world title in balance beam. The event showed that the United States had two of the best gymnasts in the world. Talk of a rivalry swirled. The two gymnasts remained friends outside of the gym. They hoped to work together to lead Team USA to an Olympic gold medal. But they both knew only one of them could leave Beijing with the all-around title.

American gymnast Shawn Johnson performs on the floor exercise during the 2008 Olympic all-around finals in Beijing, China.

An All-Around Battle

Johnson and Liukin arrived in Beijing as Team USA's stars. Their first shot at a gold medal ended in disappointment, though. The United States and China came into the Games as the two team favorites. And the teams indeed battled throughout four rotations. In the end, though, the Chinese gymnasts were too good. They put on a magnificent gold-medal-winning performance for the home crowd. Team USA won silver.

The next medal up for grabs was the all-around title. This time the rivalry was all-American. Johnson and Liukin were the clear favorites. And they went through the competition in the same rotation.

Both began on the vault. Johnson nailed a very difficult vault. Liukin's vault was simpler. But she executed it well. That included a stuck landing. Johnson ended the first rotation with the lead. The battle was on.

They moved to the uneven bars. This was Liukin's specialty. She had the edge in both difficulty and execution. Bars, meanwhile, was Johnson's weakest event. She performed her routine well. But the routine did not compare to Liukin's. The gymnasts swapped positions on the leaderboard. Next up was the balance beam.

Many gymnasts say balance beam is their least favorite event. There is little room for error on the four-inch (10-cm) beam. Any mistake can be devastating. But neither gymnast made a major mistake on this day. Each presented her routine with grace. Liukin performed slightly better. She widened her lead going into the floor exercise. A strong performance there could secure the gold medal.

Liukin performed before Johnson on floor. Her routine was set to a Russian folk melody. The performance was classically elegant. Liukin finished with a solid two and a half twist. When she hit her ending pose, she closed her eyes, savoring the moment.

Johnson was getting ready to perform as the judges calculated Liukin's score. Finally, the score showed. Johnson couldn't resist a peek at the scoreboard. Liukin had scored 15.525. That meant Johnson would need to score 16.125 to overtake her. Johnson knew that was an impossible score. Her heart sank.

"My biggest goal," she wrote later, "was out of reach."

Johnson couldn't win gold. But she knew she could still win a medal with a great routine. She threw herself into her tumbling with more than her usual gusto. The performance drew cheers with every landing. The routine ended up being one of the best Johnson had ever done. She ran off the floor and was greeted with a hug from Liukin. A moment later Johnson's score was posted. It was just below Liukin in second place. The two friends and competitors had taken gold and silver.

The moment was a milestone in US gymnastics. Never before had US gymnasts taken the top two all-around spots at an Olympics. Johnson and Liukin knew they had accomplished something very special. And both would go on to win multiple individual medals, as well. Johnson claimed the top prize in the individual balance beam and a silver medal in floor exercise. Liukin added silver medals on the uneven bars and balance beam and a bronze medal on floor.

8

London 2012
GABBY'S GOLDEN MOMENT

Gabby Douglas had a long journey to make the 2012 US Olympic team. Literally. She had grown up in Virginia Beach, Virginia. And she quickly became one of the best gymnasts in her area. But by 2010, she felt something wasn't quite right. Douglas felt she needed a different coach to help her reach the Olympic Games. She knew just the one. Liang Chow had coached 2008 Olympian Shawn Johnson. Unfortunately, Chow's gym was more than 1,000 miles (1,609 km) away in Iowa.

US gymnast Gabby Douglas soars high above the bar on a release move during the 2012 Olympic all-around final in London, England.

Douglas begged her mother to let her move to Iowa to work with Chow. It took some time to convince Douglas's mother. But eventually, her older siblings chimed in. Let Gabby go to Iowa, they said. Let her try to achieve her dream. Eventually, her mother agreed.

It was not easy for Douglas to be separated from her family. Des Moines, Iowa, was very different from Virginia Beach. Douglas often felt alone. Chow was a kind man. But he demanded the most from his gymnasts. It took all of Douglas's strength to get through each practice. But she improved rapidly. And her progress did not go unnoticed.

The American Cup is one of the biggest meets each year. And it attracts some of the biggest stars in the world. The meet also had a history of predicting Olympic success. Comaneci had won the first American Cup in 1976. Several months later, she won Olympic gold. That same thing happened with Mary Lou Retton and Nastia Liukin. So US national team coordinator Martha Karolyi arranged for Douglas to get a last-minute invite to compete there.

There was a catch. Douglas was an alternate. That meant her scores did not show up in the record book. But she still performed in all four events. Douglas lit up Madison Square Garden in New York City with her bright smile. And she flew through her routines, hitting landings.

Liang Chow cheers on Gabby Douglas as she performs at the
2012 Olympic Games.

The judges were impressed. Jordyn Wieber won the all-around title. But Douglas actually had a higher all-around score. She was officially on her way to gymnastics stardom.

The Star of London

Douglas continued to improve all summer. She fell just short of Wieber at the US championships. But Douglas finally overtook Wieber at the US Olympic Trials. That officially secured Douglas's spot on the Olympic team.

Gabby Douglas performs on the balance beam during the all-around finals at the 2012 Olympic Games.

The 16-year-old joined Wieber, McKayla Maroney, Aly Raisman, and Kyla Ross to make up Team USA. The group traveled to London, England, with high expectations.

The Olympic competition began with the preliminary round. Four gymnasts from each country competed in each event. The top three scores counted toward the team qualifications. Meanwhile, as many as two gymnasts per country could advance to the individual finals. The United States had three very good all-around gymnasts in Douglas, Raisman, and Wieber. But only two could make the all-around finals.

There were no guarantees that one would be Douglas. Wieber was the defending world champion. Raisman was the team's sturdy veteran. Douglas, meanwhile, tended to be a little wobbly on beam during big meets.

The US women did their job in the team qualification. Team USA qualified for the team finals with the highest score. The all-around race was bittersweet, however. Russia's Viktoria Komova qualified in first place. Raisman finished second. And in third, Douglas barely edged Wieber.

Fierce Gold

All great teams need a nickname. So the 2012 US Olympic women's gymnasts started to think of ideas. Someone suggested "The Fierce Five." The sassy name stuck. Throughout the competition, each gymnast did her best to help the team live up to its name. It did. The Americans presented a nearly mistake-free performance in the team competition. The result was hardly dramatic. Team USA won the gold medal over Russia and Romania. The United States has had many great individual gymnasts over the years. However, the Fierce Five became only the second US women's team to win the gold medal. The first was "The Magnificent Seven" in 1996.

That meant Douglas would move on to the finals. The defending world champion had finished fourth. Yet she was done in the all-around.

The all-around quickly turned into a contest among four gymnasts. They were Douglas, Raisman, Komova, and fellow Russian Aliya Mustafina. Komova drifted to the side while landing her difficult Amanar vault that includes one flip and two and a half twists. That allowed Douglas to take an early lead. But Komova made up ground on the uneven bars. Next up was the balance beam. Douglas came back with a wonderful performance there. Meanwhile, Raisman and Mustafina both fell. That put the spotlight on Douglas and Komova going into the final rotation.

Douglas held the lead after three events. She then performed her floor exercise routine. Known as "The Flying Squirrel," Douglas exploded with back-to-back tumbling runs. The crowd was behind her. Fans clapped along to her music. At the end of her routine, a huge smile lit up her face. But she still had to wait for Komova.

Komova also performed an excellent routine. But it proved to be not quite enough. Douglas had won the gold medal. And in doing so, she became the first black gymnast to win the Olympic women's all-around title.

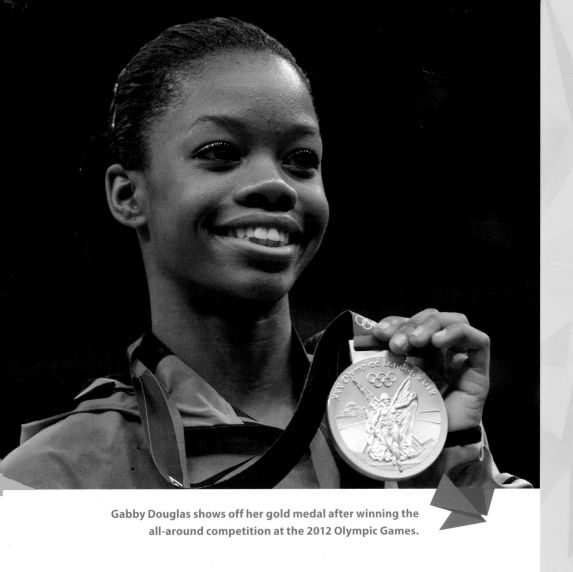

Gabby Douglas shows off her gold medal after winning the all-around competition at the 2012 Olympic Games.

Winning the medal dramatically changed Douglas's life. She was a huge star in the United States. Bela Karolyi had earned a reputation as one of gymnastics' all-time great coaches. Even he was impressed by Douglas's showing. "She came out of nowhere and was an explosion, boom!" he said. "She's going to be huge, huge."

Great Olympians

Nikolai Andrianov (Soviet Union)

The leader of the 1970s Soviet men's teams that toppled the long-standing Japanese dynasty, he won 15 Olympic medals.

Nadia Comaneci (Romania)

Nadia Comaneci was the first woman to score a perfect 10 in Olympic gymnastics competition. She won three gold medals, a silver, and a bronze at the 1976 Games.

Alexander Dityatin (Soviet Union)

He won a medal in every single event at the 1980 Olympics. He took gold in the individual all-around, rings, and team competition.

Sawao Kato (Japan)

The 1968 and 1972 Olympic all-around champion helped the Japanese men dominate gymnastics during the 1960s and 1970s. Kato earned eight gold medals in Olympic competition.

Olga Korbut (Soviet Union)

The darling of the 1972 Games was a daring gymnast who introduced several new moves on uneven bars and balance beam. Her charming performances made her a household name.

Larisa Latynina (Soviet Union)

This graceful Soviet won a total of 18 Olympic medals at the 1956, 1960, and 1964 Olympics. Nine of them were gold.

Mary Lou Retton (USA)

The spirited American star vaulted into history at the 1984 Olympics, earning a perfect 10 to clinch the all-around gold.

Vitaly Scherbo (Unified Team/Belarus)

At the 1992 Olympics, "The Man From Minsk" won an incredible six gold medals, out of a possible eight.

Glossary

BOYCOTT
To refuse participation as a form of protest.

COMPULSORY EXERCISES
Identical routines that each gymnast must perform.

DISMOUNT
The last acrobatic move in a routine. On bars, beam, and vault, the gymnast comes off the apparatus and lands on a mat.

GAYLORD
A release move on the high bar named after US gymnast Mitch Gaylord. A double flip with a half twist is completed before re-grasping the bar.

KOVACS
A release move on the high bar in which the gymnast flips twice before recatching the bar.

RELEASE MOVE
A move performed on the uneven bars or high bar in which a gymnast lets go of the bar, performs a move, and re-catches the bar without the feet touching the ground.

SPRINGBOARD
A piece of equipment that gives a gymnast extra bounce to mount the vaulting table or the uneven bars.

STUCK LANDING
The act of landing a dismount on one's feet and not moving at all is "sticking" the landing.

VAULTING TABLE
The padded table that gymnasts push off of with their hands on vault.

YURCHENKO
A vault that begins with a roundoff onto a springboard, followed by a back handspring or handspring with a full twist onto the vaulting table and a flip, sometimes twisting, off the table.

For More
Information

SELECTED BIBLIOGRAPHY

Douglas, Gabrielle, and Michelle Burford. *Grace, Gold, and Glory: My Leap of Faith.* Grand Rapids, MI: Zondervan, 2012.

Johnson, Shawn, and Nancy French. *Winning Balance: What I've Learned So Far About Love, Faith, and Living Your Dreams.* Carol Stream, IL: Tyndale House, 2012.

Karolyi, Bela, and Nancy Ann Richardson. *Feel No Fear: The Power, Passion, and Politics of a Life in Gymnastics.* New York: Hyperion, 1994.

Retton, Mary Lou, Bela Karolyi, and John Powers. *Mary Lou: Creating an Olympic Champion.* New York: McGraw-Hill, 1985.

Strug, Kerri, and John Lopez. *Landing on My Feet: A Diary of Dreams.* Kansas City, MO: Andrews McMeel, 1997.

FURTHER READINGS

Comaneci, Nadia. *Letters to a Young Gymnast.* New York: Basic Books, 2004.

Daggett, Tim, and Jean M. Stone. *Dare to Dream/Tragedy and Triumph: The Heroic Struggle of an Olympic Champion.* Tarrytown, NY: Wynwood Press, 1992.

Miller, Shannon, and Nancy Ann Richardson. *Winning Every Day: Gold Medal Advice for a Happy, Healthy Life.* New York: Bantam Books, 1998.

Raducan, Andreea. *The Other Side of the Medal.* New York: Wiseman, 2012.

WEBSITES

To learn more about Great Moments in Olympic Sports, visit **booklinks.abdopublishing.com**. These links are routinely monitored and updated to provide the most current information available.

PLACES TO VISIT

The Olympic Museum
Quai d'Ouchy 1
1006 Lausanne
Switzerland
+41 21 621 65 11
www.olympic.org/museum
Renovated in 2013, the Olympic Museum in the Olympic city of Lausanne, Switzerland, houses important Olympic memorabilia for all sports, including gymnastics. Visitors will also find a treasure trove of historical archives and interactive exhibits for each Olympic Games.

US Olympic Training Center
1750 E Boulder St.
Colorado Springs, CO 80909
(719) 866-4618
www.teamusa.org
The US Olympic team has welcomed more than 1.6 million visitors to its headquarters in Colorado Springs, Colorado. In addition to extensive training facilities for elite athletes, the USOTC offers visitors the chance to discover US Olympic history through its indoor and outdoor exhibitions and installations. Walking tours are conducted daily.

Index

ABOUT THE AUTHOR

Blythe Lawrence fell in love with gymnastics when she was eight years old and watching the 1992 Olympics in Barcelona, Spain. She has written about gymnastics for Universal Sports, espnW, *The Seattle Times*, and Examiner.com. Blythe would like to dedicate this book to her mother Carole, father Rex, and brother William, with thanks for all their love and encouragement.